FOAL & FRIENDS
A B C

Brittany Bennett

Foal & Friends ABC

Copyright © 2018 by Brittany Bennett

Cover photo by Bob Langrish
Author photo by Jeanne Sherman Photography

All rights reserved. No part of this book may be reproduced, distributed, or transmitted in any form or by any means, including photocopying, recording, digital scanning, or other electronic or mechanical methods, without written permission of the author.

Published 2018
Printed in the United States of America

ISBN 978-1-939294-54-8

Published by splatteredinkpress.com

splattered ink press

For my two "Horse Crazy" kids
Nate & Abby

In memory of Joan

Did you know there is a horse breed for every letter in the alphabet?

There are many more, but in this book you will be introduced to twenty-six horse breeds from around the world, each starting with a different letter of the alphabet. Horse Crazy Kids will learn their letters along with mama mare and her sweet foal. Included are some of the most popular breeds, along with those considered rare.

Those breeds currently on watch lists put together by The Livestock Conservancy and The Rare Breeds Survival Trust are Belgian Draft, Clydesdale, Lipizzan, Rocky Mountain Horses, and the Eriskay, Exmoor and New Forest Ponies.

The people who care for each equine breed have come together to raise awareness and help you learn your A, B, C's. If you see a breed and would like additional information, you can visit breed websites to discover ways to participate.

***

"These breeds are a living, breathing part of our history and the connection between humans and horses goes back thousands of years."
    ~The Livestock Conservancy

"Many of the UK's native breeds of equines are falling in numbers, as people are not aware of the importance of keeping a purebred horse or pony rather than a crossbreed. RBST is working to help people value the great temperaments and intelligence of our purebred native breeds."
    ~Rare Breeds Survival Trust

Aa is for Arabian Horse

Bb is for Belgian Draft Horse

Cc is for Clydesdale Horse

Dd is for Dutch Warmblood Horse

Ee is for Eriskay Pony

Ff

is for Fjord Horse
(Fee-Yord)

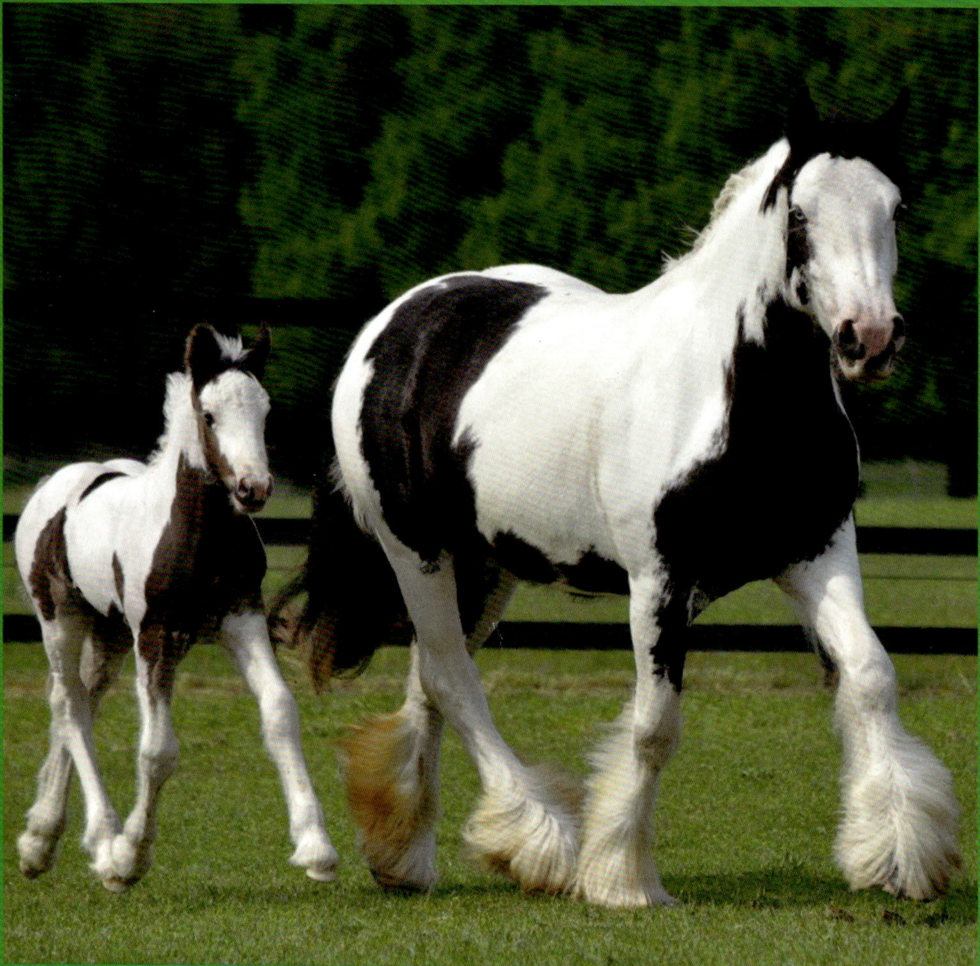

Gg

is for Gypsy Vanner Horse

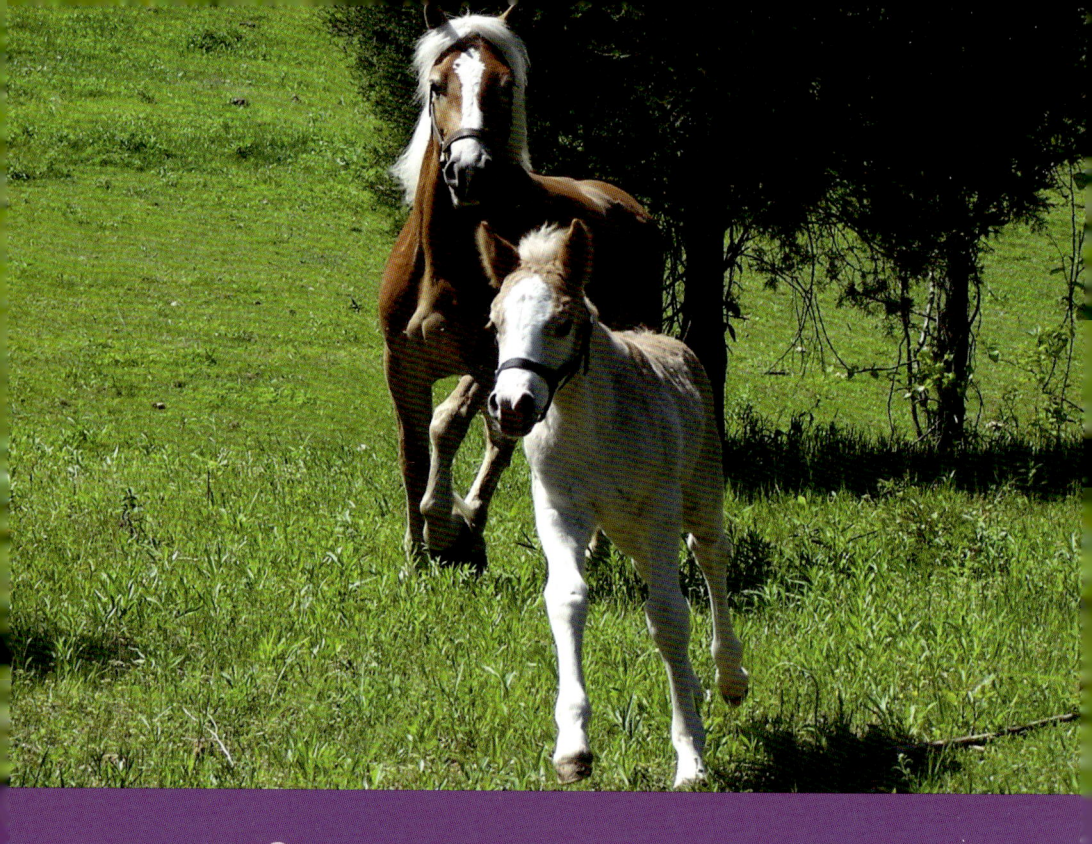

Hh is for Haflinger Horse

Ii

is for Icelandic Horse

Jj

is for Jutland Horse

Kk is for Knabstrupper Horse
(Nob-Strooper)

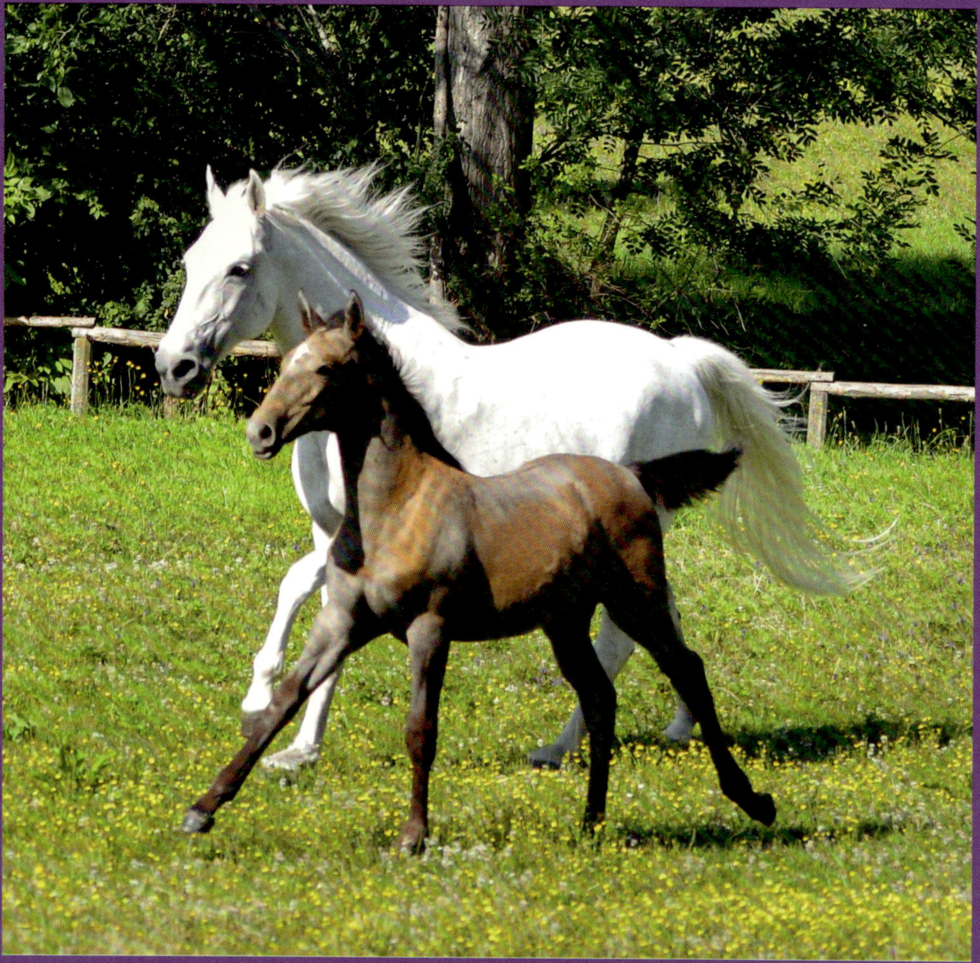

Ll

is for Lipizzan Horse

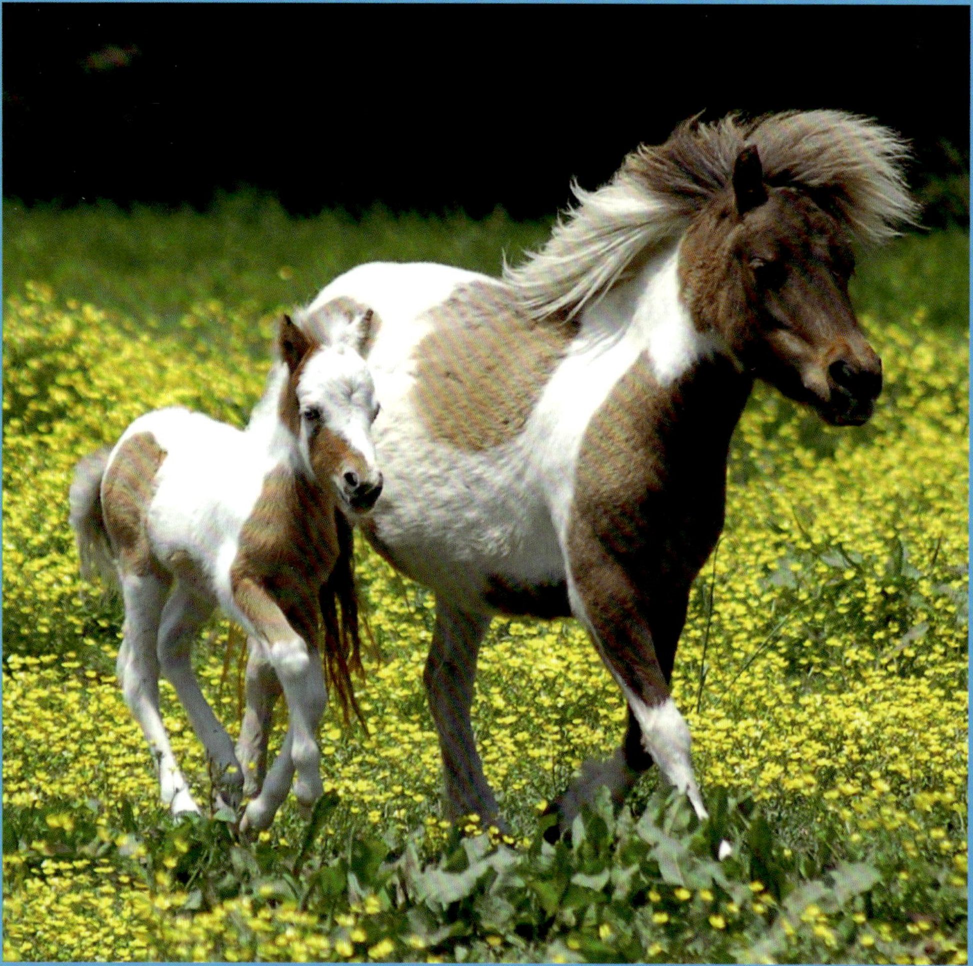

Mm

is for Miniature Horse

Nn is for New Forest Pony

Oo is for Oberlander Horse

Pp

is for Paint Horse

Qq is for Quarter Horse

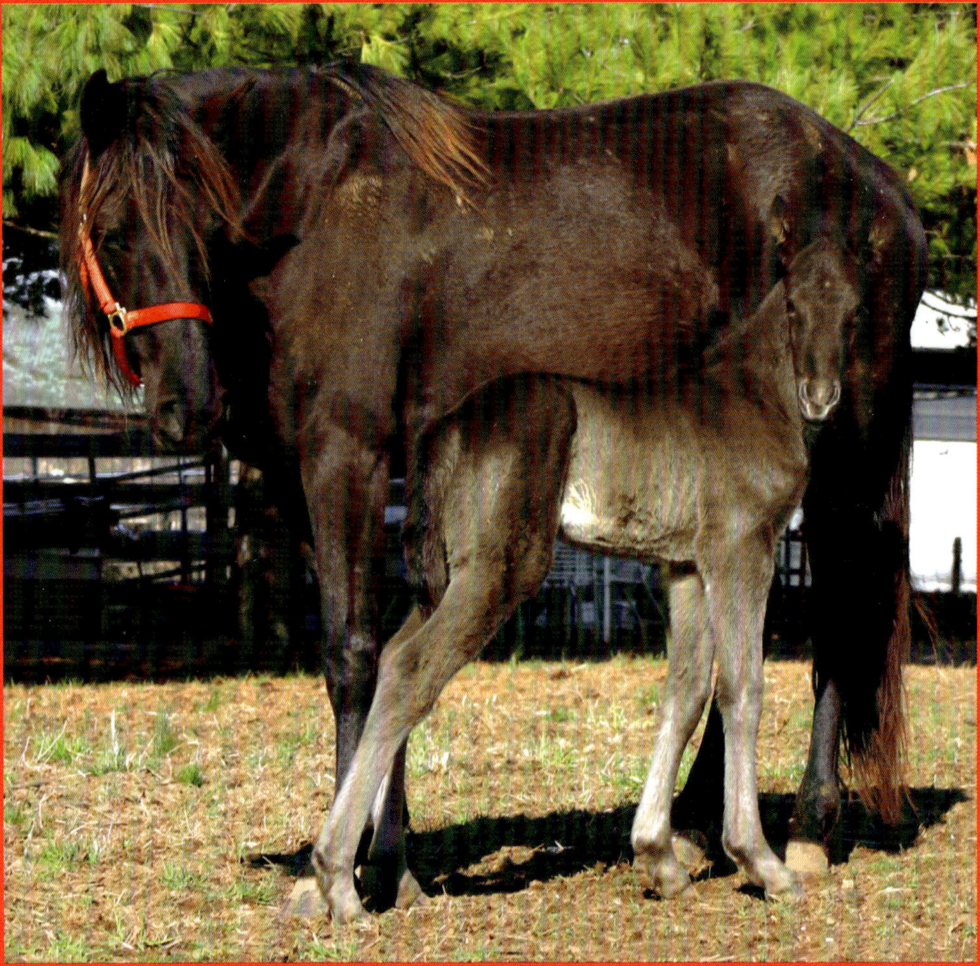

Rr

is for Rocky Mountain Horse

Ss is for Saddlebred Horse

Tt is for Thoroughbred Horse

Uu is for Ukrainian Riding Horse

Vv is for Vyatka Horse

Ww is for Welsh Pony

Xx is for EXmoor Pony

Yy is for Yakutian Horse
(Yaku-tia)

Zz is for Zebra-Burchell Horse

Thank you to everyone that made "Horse Breeds ABC" possible:

Linda Mehney - Owner/Manager
Brittany Noffsinger - Photographer

Belgian Draft Horse

Compliments of Geers Farm
Joan Geers - Photographer

Michelle Randolph - Photograph

Dutch Warmblood Horse

Anonymous Donor

Eriskay Pony

© Bob Langrish

Dun Darling Norwegian
Fjord Horses & American
Miniature Horses
Karen Sholten Maas
Owner/Photographer

N'Co Gypsy Vanners
Owner/Breeder/Photographer
www.vanners.org
www.ncogypsyvanners.com

Photo Courtesy of the American
Haflinger Registry - Kerri Durner

Icelandic Horse Association
Great Britain
Mic Rushen - Photographer

Jutland Horse

© Bob Langrish

Knabstrupper Horse

© Bob Langrish

SPANISCHE HOFREITSCHULE BUNDESGESTÜT PIBER

© Spanische Hofreitschule – Bundesgestüt Piber GöR

Photo by Sandy Revard
Mini Equine Photography

Photography Credit
Barbara J. Nelson
Stonefield Sportponies

Oberlander Horse

Photographer
Jennifer Kaffenbarger
Spur Acres, Byron IL

Photography Credit
ssican Hein/American Paint
Horse Association
www.apha.com

Christine Hamilton - Photographer
AQHA - Image Provider
Terry Crofoot of Crofoot Ranches
Breeder of both horses

Acandiana's DOBBIN 777 Mare
and Foal picture by Noemi LeBlanc

Photos by Farrell

Photo Credit:
@BarbaraBerens.com

Svetlana Golubenko - Photograph
"Universal" Stud - Owner

Alfa Horse Ltd
Vyatka Horse
Olga Koshaeva - Photographer
Tylovay, LLC - Owner

Janice Thompson - Photographer

Susan Baker - Photographer

Yakutian Horse

Photograph provided by
Nikita Zimov
Director of Pleistocene Park

Zebra-Burchell Horse

© Bob Langrish

Friesian Horse - Cover Photo

Consultant - Karen Szymas-C
& Gary Orr - Owner/Operator
HPF & HPF Equine Assisted
Riding Programs

Aa Bb Cc Dd Ee
Ff Gg Hh Ii Jj Kk
Ll Mm Nn Oo Pp
Qq Rr Ss Tt Uu
Vv Ww Xx Yy Zz

About the Author

Brittany Bennett lives in West Michigan with her two horse crazy kids. Twins, Nate and Abby, are the inspiration behind Foal and Friends, a series she wrote for her children. They have been riding since they were three years old. In an effort to learn more about horse breeds, she discovered there was a horse breed for every letter in the alphabet.

A lifelong love of horses herself, she volunteers at Renew Therapeutic Riding Center in Holland, Michigan for special needs children and adults. She has witnessed horses positively change peoples lives. We have a lot to learn from horses.